Tatsuki Fujimoto

I love chainsaws!

Tatsuki Fujimoto won Honorable Mention in the
November 2013 Shueisha Crown Newcomers' Awards for
his debut one-shot story ... 's first series,
... Man began
... *Jump*.

1

SHONEN JUMP Manga Edition

Story & Art **TATSUKI FUJIMOTO**

Translation/AMANDA HALEY
Touch-Up Art & Lettering/SABRINA HEEP
Design/JULIAN [JR] ROBINSON
Editor/ALEXIS KIRSCH

First published in Japan in 2018 by SHUEISHA Inc., Tokyo.
English translation rights arranged by SHUEISHA Inc.

Printed in the U.S.A.

Published by VIZ Media, LLC
P.O. Box 77010
San Francisco, CA 94107

11
First printing, October 2020
Eleventh printing, April 2022

SHONEN JUMP

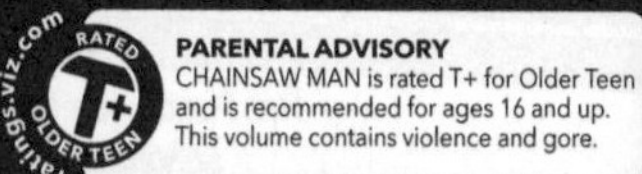

CHAINSAW MAN

1

DOG AND CHAINSAW

Tatsuki Fujimoto

CONTENTS

Chapter 1: Dog & Chainsaw

KILLING JUST ONE DEVIL...
BBROOM
...NETS ME ABOUT 300,000.
YUP, BEIN' A DEVIL HUNTER IS THE BEST WAY TO MAKE SOME MOOLA.

Chapter 1: Dog & Chainsaw

Chain saw man

THIS ONE'S A *TOMATO DEVIL,* SIR.

IT'LL COME BACK FROM THE SEEDS, SO YOU SHOULD BURN IT.

AFTER I USE THIS TO PAY THE WATER BILL...

PLUS THE DEBTS I'VE GOT TO OTHER PEOPLE...

THAT'S FUNNY.
I'M ALREADY DOWN TO 1,800 YEN...

GOT NOTHING TO EAT AT HOME...
WE HAVE TO LIVE ON THIS FOR THE REST OF THE MONTH...

OKAY, POCHITA.
OUR MEAL FOR THE DAY IS A SINGLE SLICE OF BREAD.

WHY ARE WE EMPLOYING SOME KID AS A DEVIL HUNTER?

WE'RE MAKING HIM PAY BACK HIS DEBT TO US.
MORE ACCURATELY, HIS WORTHLESS DEAD DAD'S DEBT.

IS A KID WITH A PET DEVIL REALLY FIT TO BE A DEVIL HUNTER?

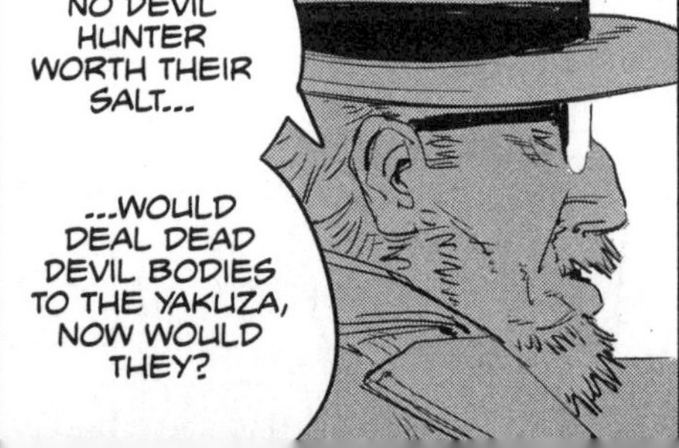
NO DEVIL HUNTER WORTH THEIR SALT...
...WOULD DEAL DEAD DEVIL BODIES TO THE YAKUZA, NOW WOULD THEY?

PLUS, WHAT'S NICE ABOUT DENJI IS HE ALWAYS DOES AS HE'S TOLD.

HEY, FIDO! I'LL GIVE YOU 100 YEN TO EAT THIS CIG!

You mean it, sir?!
Down the hatch!

gulp
AH HA HA HA HA HA!

WE'LL CALL YOU AGAIN THE NEXT TIME THERE'S A DEVIL.
AND REMEMBER, IF YOU RUN AWAY, YOU'LL BE PIG SLOP!

bleh

NOW WE'LL BE ABLE TO EAT FOR THE NEXT *THREE DAYS!*

ZSSHHHH

I HEARD SOMETHING RECENTLY...
APPARENTLY, IT'S NORMAL TO EAT YOUR SLICED BREAD WITH JAM ON IT.
WELL, "NORMAL" IS JUST A PIPE DREAM FOR US, ANYWAY.
FEELS LIKE I'LL BE PAYING OFF MY DEBT TILL THE DAY I DIE.

Whiiiiine

AND I'LL PROLLY NEVER GET TO GO OUT WITH A GIRL.
CAN'T ASK A GIRL OVER TO MY RUN-DOWN SHACK, AND I DON'T GOT MONEY FOR A DATE EITHER.

IF DREAMS DO COME TRUE, I WANNA HUG A GIRL BEFORE I DIE...

HHHSSSS

SSSHHHH

BASTARD HUNG HIMSELF WITHOUT MAKING THIS MONTH'S PAYMENT...

KID... I DON'T CARE IF YOU BEG FOR IT OR WHORE YOURSELF OUT. HAVE 700,000 YEN READY BY TOMORROW.
OR I'LL CUT YOUR CORPSE INTO PIECES AND SELL YOU.

BRUMM
A CH-CHAIN-SAW?!
BRM BRM-BRM
BRM
IT'S A DEVIL!
IF YOU'RE GONNA KILL ME, GET IT OVER WITH!
I'M GONNA DIE ANYWAY!

YOU'RE HURT...
ARE YOU GONNA DIE TOO...?

BITE ME!
I HEARD THAT IF A DEVIL DRINKS BLOOD, ITS WOUNDS HEAL!
IF YOU DON'T WANNA DIE, THEN BITE ME!
CHOMP
MY BLOOD DOESN'T COME FREE...
THIS IS A CONTRACT...

I'LL SAVE YOU... SO YOU SAVE ME.
I DON'T WANNA DIE EITHER...
WILL YOU HIRE ME AS A DEVIL HUNTER, SIR?
SPLORCH

SO HUNGRY I CAN'T SLEEP...

WHEN I CAN'T SLEEP, I THINK ABOUT MY DEBT, AND THEN IT'S EVEN HARDER TO FALL ASLEEP...

OH, I KNOW...
THIS IS WHAT I'LL DREAM OF WHEN I FALL ASLEEP TONIGHT...

I'LL SPREAD JAM ON SLICED BREAD AND EAT IT WITH YOU.

I'LL FLIRT AND STUFF WITH A GIRL.

WE'LL PLAY VIDEO GAMES IN OUR ROOM TOGETHER...

...AND I'LL FALL ASLEEP IN HER ARMS...

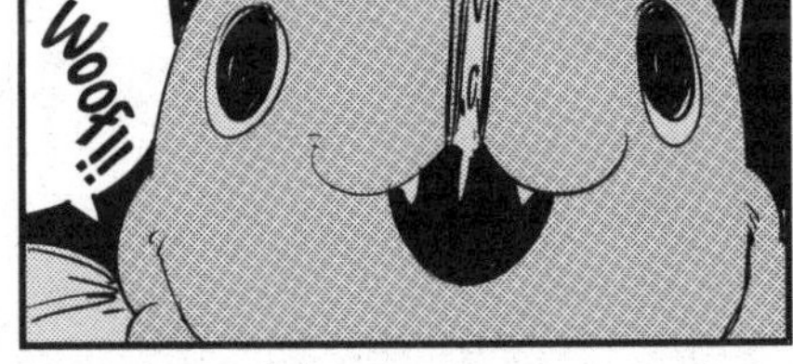

BLEUGH
Warf?!
BAM BAM

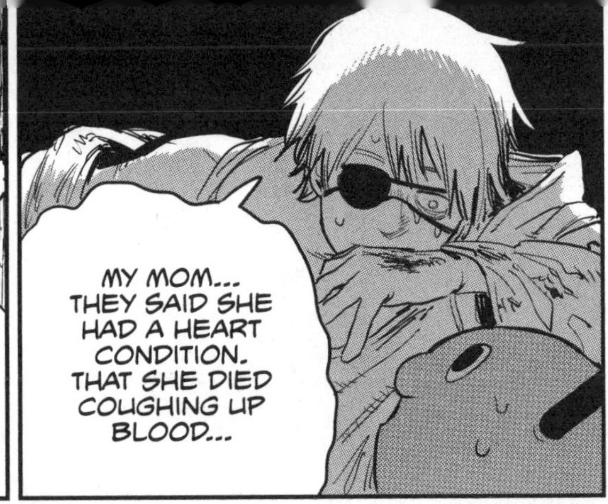
MY MOM... THEY SAID SHE HAD A HEART CONDITION. THAT SHE DIED COUGHING UP BLOOD...

tak tak
DENJI! GOT A DEVIL.
TIME FOR WORK.

WISH THEY'D AT LEAST LET ME DREAM...

A DEVIL SHOWED UP *HERE*, SIR?

I DON'T SEE IT...
MAYBE IT HID SOME-WHERE?

DENJI, BOY... WE'RE GRATEFUL TO YOU, Y'KNOW.

OH, UH... YES, SIR...

YOU'RE OBE-DIENT LIKE A DOG...
...AND YOU WORK FOR CHEAP TREATS LIKE ONE TOO.

UH-HUH...

THING IS... I HATE DOGS. CAN'T STAND THE SMELL.

rstl

SHM
P

WE YAKUZA BOYS...

WE WANTED TO GET STRONGER TOO. TO MAKE MORE MONEY.
SO WE DECIDED TO DO LIKE YOU AND MAKE OUR OWN DEAL WITH A DEVIL.

WHAT WE WANT IS THE DEVILS' POWER...
AND WHAT I WANT IS THE DEATHS...
...OF ALL DEVIL HUNTERS!

HEY, LITTLE DEVIL HUNTERRR!
THESE GUYS! THEY'RE SERIOUSLY STUPID! TOTAL SUCKERS!
WHEN I SAID I'D GIVE THEM MY DEVIL POWER...
...THEY BECAME MY SLAVES FREAKIN' WILLINGLY!
TOO BAD MY POWER TURNS PEOPLE INTO ZOMBIES!
CUZ I'M THE ZOMBIE DEVIL!

DEVIL HUNTERS KILL US DEVILS. I HATE THEM!!
SO I KILL THEM!
YOU GUYS! CUT HIM INTO PIECES AND DUMP 'IM IN THE GARBAGE!

DASH

JUST DREAMING OF A NORMAL LIFE WAS ENOUGH FOR ME.
DO I NOT EVEN GET TO HAVE THAT MUCH?

D40

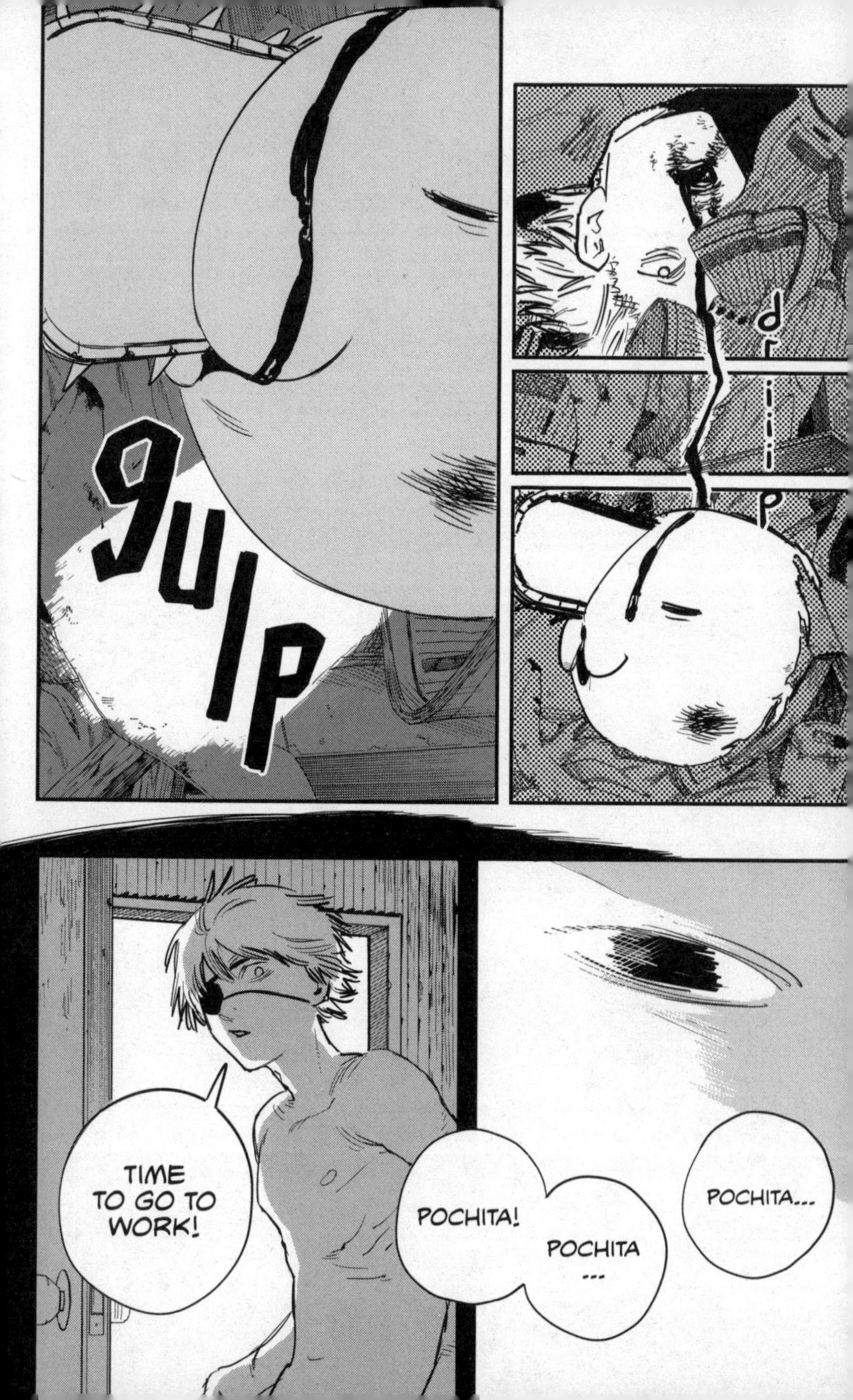

driiip

gulp

POCHITA...

POCHITA ...

POCHITA!

TIME TO GO TO WORK!

VREEEEE

POCHITA ...

I MIGHT DIE WHILE I'M FIGHTING DEVILS.

IF I DO, YOU'LL BE MY ONE REGRET.

I HEARD SOME DEVILS CAN TAKE OVER DEAD BODIES.

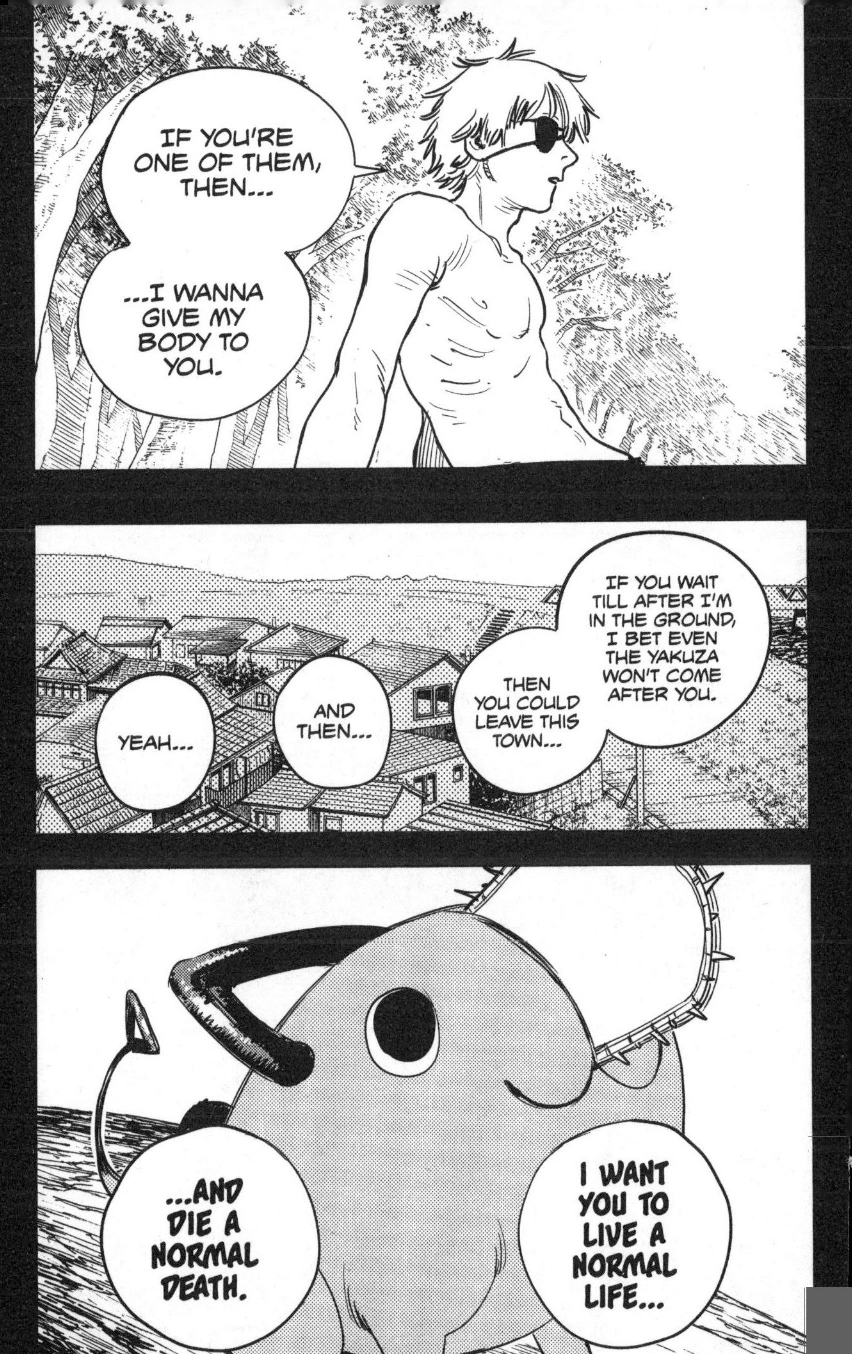
IF YOU'RE ONE OF THEM, THEN...
...I WANNA GIVE MY BODY TO YOU.
IF YOU WAIT TILL AFTER I'M IN THE GROUND, I BET EVEN THE YAKUZA WON'T COME AFTER YOU.
THEN YOU COULD LEAVE THIS TOWN...
AND THEN...
YEAH...
I WANT YOU TO LIVE A NORMAL LIFE...
...AND DIE A NORMAL DEATH.

MAKE MY DREAMS COME TRUE FOR ME!

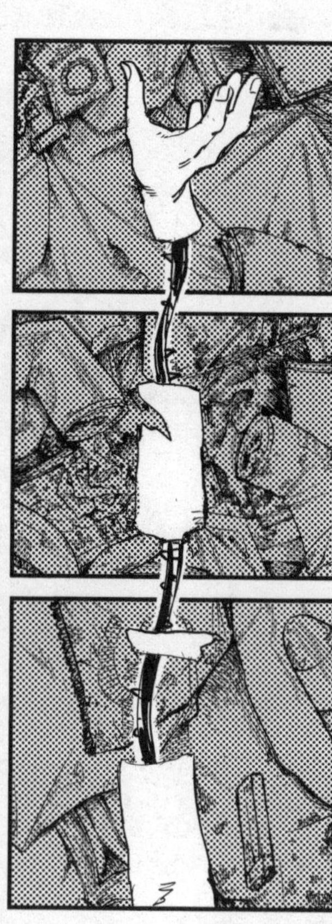

Woof
!!!

POCHITA
...
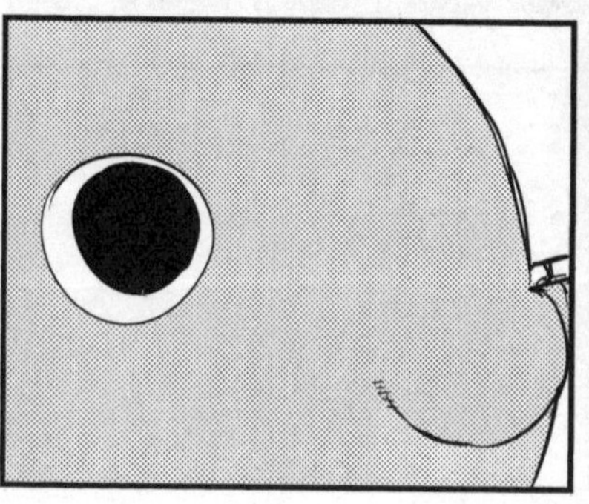

DID YOU TAKE MY BODY? LIKE I TOLD YOU TO?

I'VE ALWAYS...
...LOVED LISTENING TO YOU TALK ABOUT YOUR DREAMS.

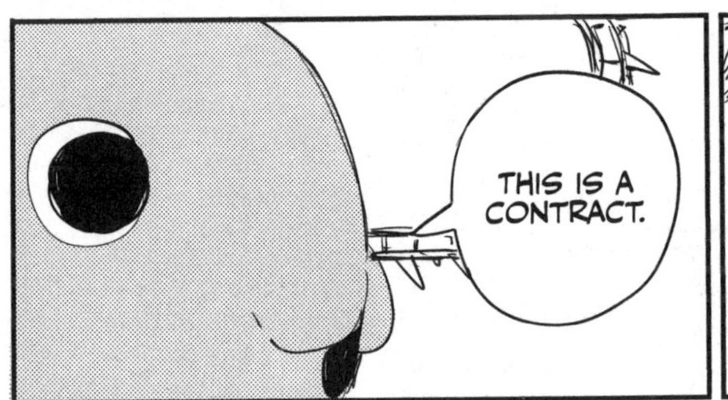
THIS IS A CONTRACT.

I'LL GIVE YOU MY HEART.
IN EXCHANGE ...

...SHOW ME YOUR DREAMS.

POCHITA!

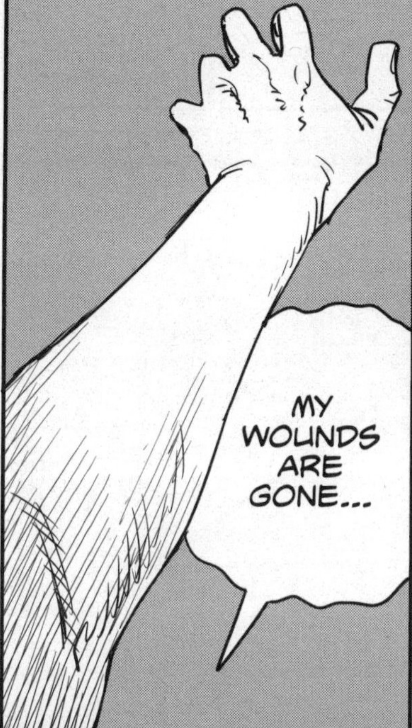
MY WOUNDS ARE GONE...

POCHITA!

HUH?

WE CUT HIM TO RIBBONS AND HE'S STILL ALIVE?!
GROSS!
I *REALLY* HATE DEVIL HUNTERS!

YOU GUYS!! EAT THAT FREAK!!

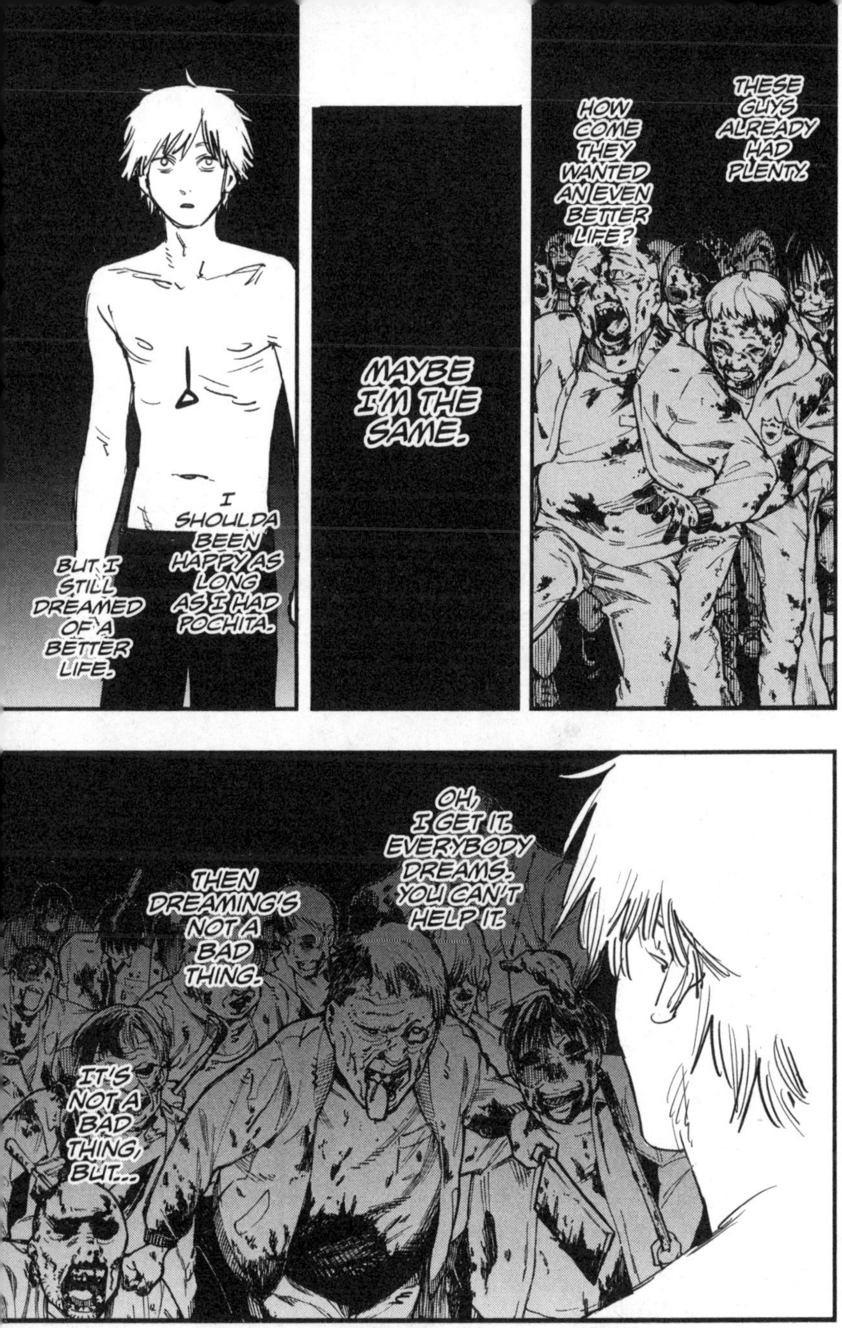

THESE GUYS ALREADY HAD PLENTY.
HOW COME THEY WANTED AN EVEN BETTER LIFE?

MAYBE I'M THE SAME.

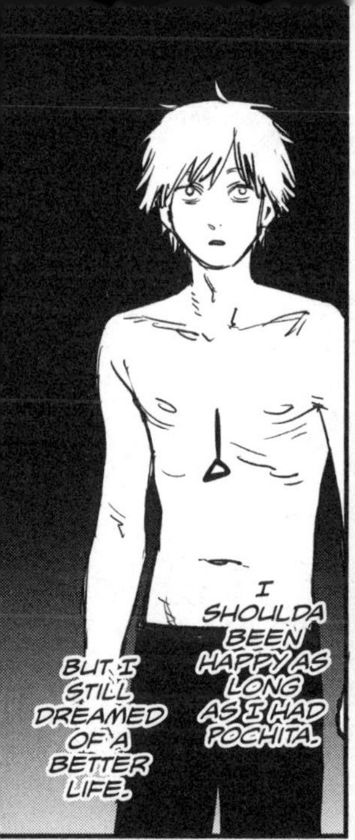
I SHOULDA BEEN HAPPY AS LONG AS I HAD POCHITA.
BUT I STILL DREAMED OF A BETTER LIFE.

OH, I GET IT. EVERYBODY DREAMS. YOU CAN'T HELP IT.
THEN DREAMING'S NOT A BAD THING.
IT'S NOT A BAD THING, BUT...

IF YOU'RE GONNA GET IN OUR WAY...
...THEN DIE!
BDRDOM

HE *HAS* TO STAY DEAD IF WE EAT HIM...

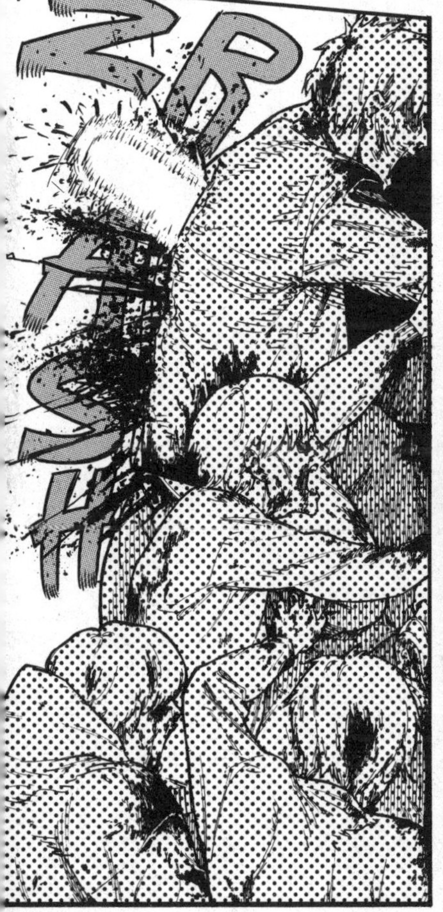
ZRASH

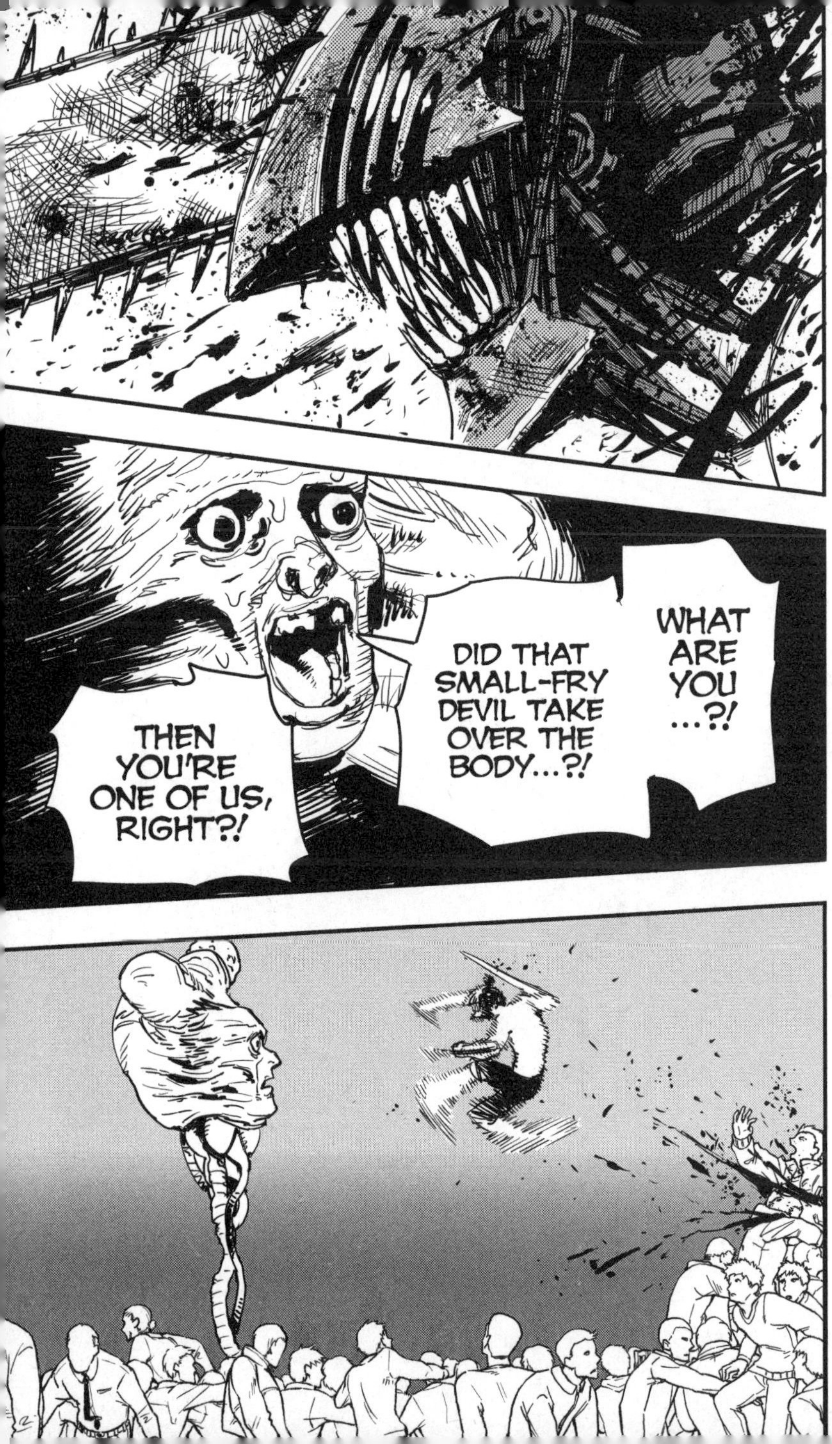

WHAT ARE YOU ...?!

DID THAT SMALL-FRY DEVIL TAKE OVER THE BODY...?!

THEN YOU'RE ONE OF US, RIGHT?!

LOOKS LIKE YOU GUYS...
...TURNED INTO DEVILS DOWN TO YOUR HEARTS.

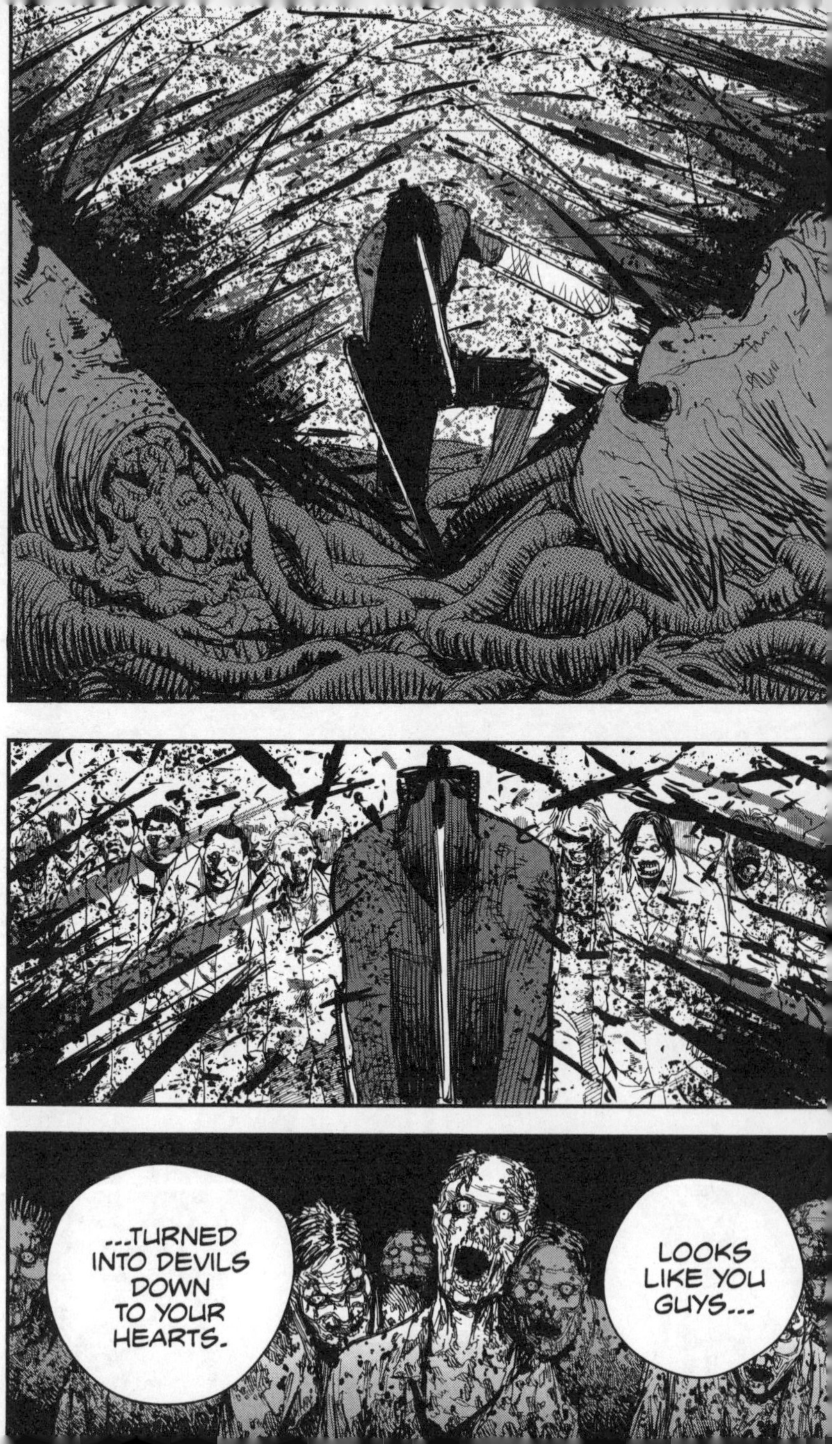

AND SINCE I GET PAID TO BE A DEVIL HUNTER...
...I GOTTA KILL DEVILS DEAD!

I KNOW!
IF I KILL EVERY LAST ONE OF YOU...
...IT'S BYE-BYE, DEBT!

GYAA HA HA HA HA!!

LOOKS LIKE SOMEONE BEAT US TO THE PUNCH.

GOT A LIVE ONE.

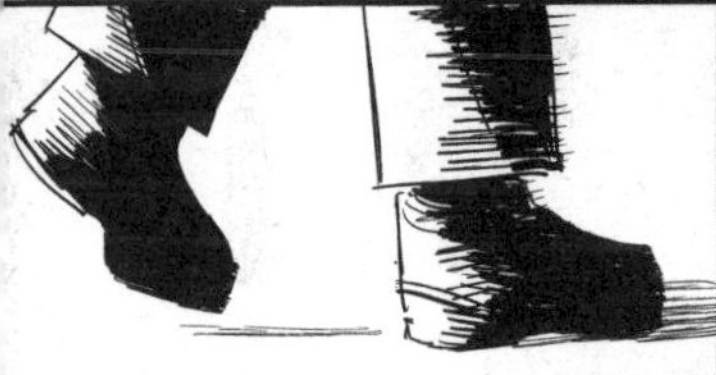

HMM...

YOU HAVE A PECULIAR SMELL.
IT ISN'T HUMAN OR DEVIL.

DID YOU DO THIS?

YOU'RE HUMAN...
ANY CHANCE IT'S A DEVIL POSSES-SION?
NONE. YOU CAN SEE POSSESSION ON THEIR FACES.

I CAME HERE TO KILL THE ZOMBIE DEVIL.
I'M A PUBLIC SAFETY DEVIL HUNTER.

YOU HAVE TWO CHOICES.
ONE, BE KILLED BY ME AS A DEVIL.
OR TWO, BE KEPT BY ME AS A HUMAN.

IF YOU'RE MY PET, I'LL GIVE YOU FOOD.

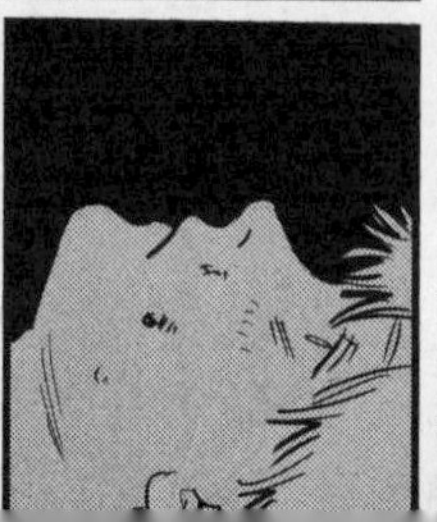

FOOD...?
WHAT WOULD I GET FOR BREAK-FAST?

LET'S SEE...
BREAD WITH BUTTER AND JAM...
SALAD, COFFEE...
AND... MAYBE DESSERT?

THAT'S A DREAM COME TRUE...

Chainsaw
man

Chapter 2: The Place Where Pochita Is

gurrrrrgle

THAT'S MY STOMACH...

SORRY, UH... I'M BROKE...

WE HAVEN'T HAD BREAKFAST EITHER.
LET'S GRAB SOME FOOD AT A REST STOP.

PICK ANYTHING YOU WANT. I'LL PAY.
Really ?!

ALSO, YOU'LL DRAW ATTENTION SHIRTLESS. PUT THIS ON.

PEOPLE ALWAYS CALL ME DIRTY AND SMELLY. NOBODY EVER COMES NEAR ME.
THIS'S THE FIRST TIME I'VE BEEN TREATED NICE.
AND BY A PRETTY GIRL, AT THAT...

I'M IN LOVE.

OH, I'LL HAVE UDON AND... UDON AND...
...A HOT DOG! IS THAT OKAY?!
SURE THING.

H—
H-HELP ME!

I'M A PUBLIC SAFETY DEVIL HUNTER, SIR.
WHAT HAP-PENED?

A D-DEVIL SNATCHED MY DAUGHTER!
MY LITTLE GIRL, IT—

IT TOOK HER INTO THE WOODS!!

CURRY UDON'S UP!

OH... THAT'S ME.

WHAT'S YOUR NAME?
IT'S DENJI!

OKAY, DENJI...
I DON'T WANT MY NOODLES TO GET SOGGY. YOU GO KILL THE DEVIL BY YOURSELF.

HUH?! UH, BUT I'M HAVING UDON TOO.

AN EXPERIENCED DEVIL HUNTER IS ON THE JOB, SIR. HE'LL SAVE YOUR DAUGHTER.
PLEASE REMAIN INSIDE THE BUILDING FOR YOUR SAFETY.
REALLY ?

DID YOU FORGET? YOU'RE MY PET.
ONLY ANSWER WITH "YES" OR "WOOF."

WH... WHAT'S THAT MEAN...?

I DON'T NEED A DOG WHO SAYS "NO."

I HEARD FROM AN ACQUAINTANCE IN THE CRIME SCENE DIVISION THAT...

...OUR USELESS DOGS GET EUTHANIZED.

I THOUGHT SHE WAS NICE.
I EVEN LIKED HER A LITTLE.
I CAN'T BELIEVE SHE WAS THAT SCARY!

TREATIN' ME LIKE A DAMN DOG...!

Woof!

I JUST REMEMBERED POCHITA'S DEAD...
BLAAAH...

Ah ha ha ha!

Ha ha ha!

AH.

OH, PLEASE! LET THIS DEVIL GO!

WAIT, WHAT?

WHEN HE WAS HITTING ME IN THE PARKING LOT TODAY...
...THIS NICE DEVIL SAVED ME!

MY DADDY... WHEN HE HAS A BAD DAY, HE BEATS ME.

SO, PLEASE! DON'T KILL HIM...

OUR USELESS DOGS GET EUTHANIZED.

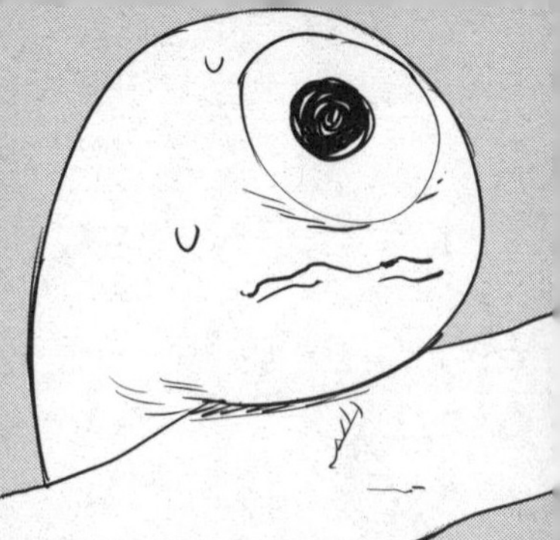

HEY... WANNA RUN AWAY TOGETHER? THE THREE OF US...?

HUH?

I WAS BUDDIES WITH A DEVIL TOO. I KNOW...
...THERE ARE GOOD DEVILS.

BUT IF I LET THIS DEVIL GO, THEY'RE GONNA KILL ME.
SO DO YOU WANNA RUN AWAY...?

AH HA!
CAN WE...?

clasp
AH HA HA HA HA!

WE TOTALLY CAN!

HA HA HA...

AH HA HA HA HA HA HA HA!

AH HA HA HA HA HA HA HA!

HA HA... HUH?

HAH! I WIN!
HA HA HA!
WHAT THE HELL IS THIS?!
I'LL SHOW YOU SOMETHING COOL BEFORE YOU DIE.
I'M THE MUSCLE DEVIL, AND THAT MEANS...

ARRGH!!
I CAN CONTROL ANY MUSCLES I'M TOUCHING!
I'M GONNA HAVE SOME FUN WITH THIS FEMALE BRAT NOW.
BEHAVE YOURSELF OVER THERE, 'KAY?
twitch
AH HA HA HA HA HA HA HA!

AH HA HA HA HA HA HA HA!
twitch
twitch
twitch
twitch
twitch
HEH HEH HEH...

EE!

WHAT A RELIEF. I WON'T FEEL BAD...
...FOR KILLING A LOWLIFE LIKE YOU.
OW OW OW OW OW OW OW OW?!

VRRR
SPSSHH

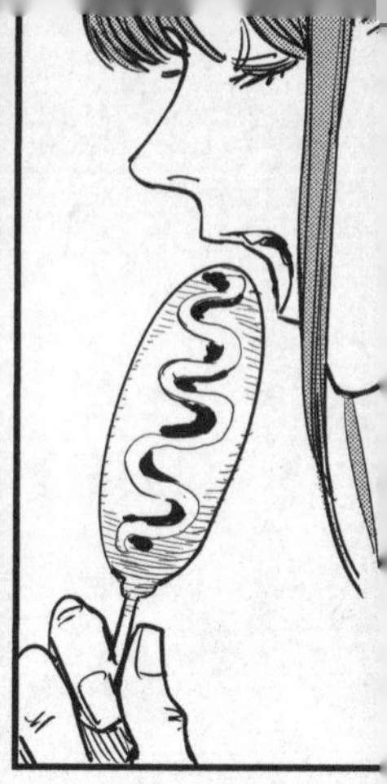

WOOF...

topple

UH-OH.
WHUMP

YOU OKAY?
SHE SMELLS GOOD...

SORRY... I END UP CUTTING MY OWN BODY WITH THE CHAINSAWS TOO...
LOOKS LIKE I LOSE TOO MUCH BLOOD AND GET FAINT...

HOW DID YOUR BODY END UP LIKE THAT?

MY PET DEVIL BECAME MY HEART.
UNBE-LIEVABLE, RIGHT?

I DON'T WANNA BELIEVE IT EITHER.
THAT POCHITA DIED FOR ME...

HISTORICALLY SPEAKING, YOUR CONDITION HAS VERY FEW PRE-CEDENTS.
SO FEW IT HASN'T EVEN BEEN NAMED.

I BELIEVE YOU.

I HAVE AN ESPECIALLY GOOD NOSE.
SO I CAN TELL.

YOUR BEST FRIEND IS STILL ALIVE INSIDE YOU.

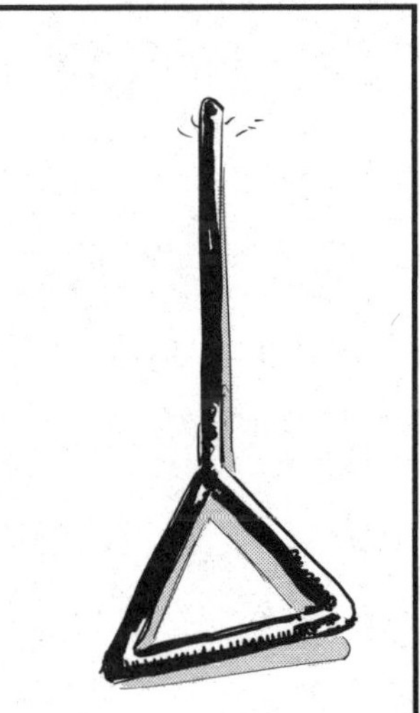
AND NOT IN THE POETIC SENSE...
YOUR BODY HAS *TWO* SCENTS. HUMAN *AND* DEVIL.

OKAY...

WOW...
THAT'S A HUGE RELIEF!

gurgle

I'LL EAT THAT UDON ...
YOU LOOK UNSTEADY.
CAN YOU FEED YOURSELF?
I CA—
I can't.

Say "Ahh."

Ahh.

GOOD?

Woof!

HARD TO BELIEVE YOU ACTUALLY ENJOYED THAT SOGGY UDON...
WHAT A GOOD BOY.
YOU REALLY ARE LIKE A DOG.

HEY, UH!
WHAT'S YOUR NAME...?
MAKIMA.

SOMEONE LIKE THIS BOY NAMED DENJI.

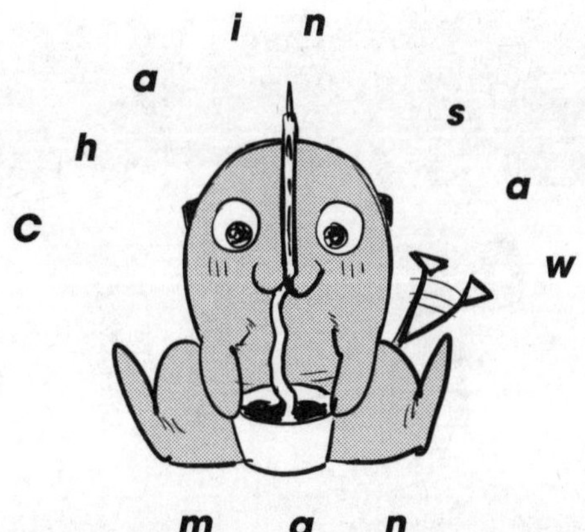
Chainsaw man

Chapter 3: Arrival in Tokyo

Chapter 3:
Arrival in Tokyo
THIS IS DEVIL HUNTER TOKYO HQ.

INCLUDING CIVILIANS, THERE ARE MORE THAN A THOUSAND DEVIL HUNTERS IN TOKYO.
WE PUBLIC SAFETY DEVIL HUNTERS...
...GET A LOT OF PAID DAYS OFF AND THE BEST BENEFITS PACKAGE.
IF MAKIMA LIKES ME, THEN...
...AS WE WORK TOGETHER, WON'T WE END UP BECOMING, YOU KNOW...?
AND IF WE'RE IN THAT KINDA RELATIONSHIP, COULDN'T WE DO THAT KINDA STUFF TOO...?
I WANNA DO IT!! I WANNA DO THAT STUFF SO BAD!!

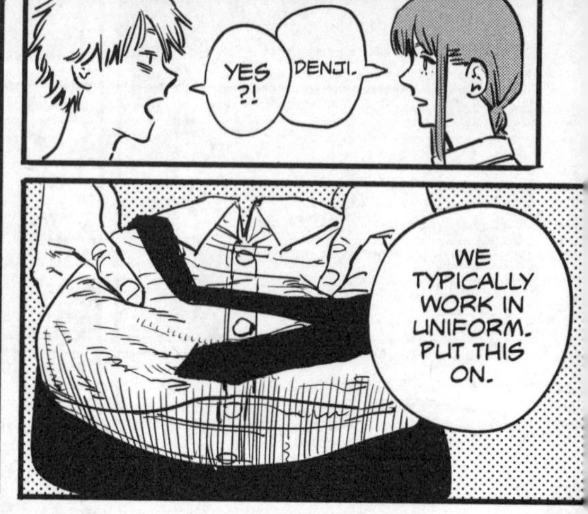
DENJI.
YES ?!
WE TYPICALLY WORK IN UNIFORM. PUT THIS ON.

ONCE YOU'RE CHANGED, I'LL INTRODUCE YOU TO ONE OF YOUR COLLEAGUES.

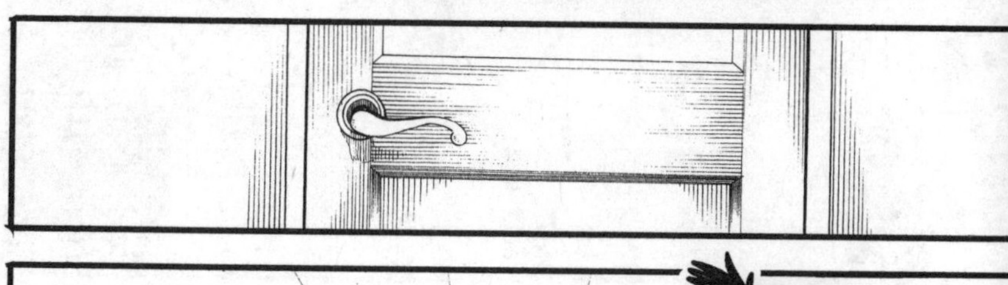

THIS IS AKI HAYAKAWA.
HE'S THREE YEARS YOUR SENIOR HERE.

FOR TODAY, TAG ALONG WITH HIM.

I'M NOT WORKING WITH YOU, MISS MAKIMA?
OF COURSE NOT.

YOU AND MISS MAKIMA ARE IN COMPLETELY DIFFERENT LEAGUES.
WE'RE GOING ON PATROL.

Nooo! Miss Maki-maaa!!

IF YOU PERFORM WELL, WE'LL BE ABLE TO WORK TOGETHER.
SO KEEP YOUR CHIN UP, OKAY?

HEY, SIR.
DOES MAKIMA HAVE A BOY-FRIEND?

HEY, TELL ME.

HEY!

C'MERE.

BAMM

WHU
D

CRA
S
H

YOU SHOULD QUIT.
IF YOU SHOW UP TOMORROW, I'LL GIVE YOU ANOTHER THRASHING.

WHAT'S YOUR PROB-LEM...?

MAYBE MY KINDNESS ISN'T GETTING THROUGH TO YOU...

THE PEOPLE WHO GO INTO THIS JOB FOR SHALLOW REASONS END UP DEAD, KID.
AMONG MY PEERS, THE ONES WHO BECAME DEVIL HUNTERS JUST FOR THE MONEY GOT KILLED BY DEVILS. ALL OF THEM.
THE ONLY ONES STILL ALIVE ARE THOSE WHO HAVE STRONG CONVICTION.

LEMME GUESS. YOU BECAME A DEVIL HUNTER CUZ YOU'VE GOT YOUR EYE ON MAKIMA?

Ding diiing.

THEN I WAS RIGHT TO BEAT YOU UP.

PTOO

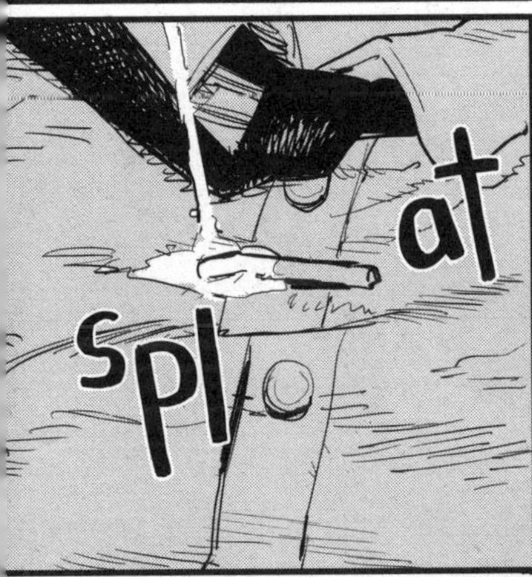
SPLAT

I'LL DO YOU A FAVOR AND TELL MAKIMA...
...YOU GOT SCARED OF A DEVIL AND RAN AWAY.

WHOMP

WHAK
WHEN I!
FIGHT!
GUYS!
I!
WHAK
ONLY!
WHAK
AIM FOR!
THE CROTCH!
WHAK
WHAK
WHAK
WHAK
WHAK

huff huff

WHEW!
TODAY, I ATE UDON FOR THE ***FIRST TIME...***
AND A HOT DOG TOO...

MAYBE I BECAME A DEVIL HUNTER FOR A REALLY SHALLOW REASON...

...BUT I'M WILLING TO *DIE* TO KEEP LIVING LIKE THIS.

GFF!

DO NG

A THUG LIKE YOU...
...HAS NO PLACE LIKING MAKIMA!

HUH?! WHAT GIVES ?!
YOU JUST WANT HER FOR YOUR-SELF!!

YOU... SERI-OUSLY ...

...ONLY AIM FOR...
...THE BALLS...

THUD

CRAP.

A TESTICLE DEVIL ATTACKED HIS BALLS.

THAT'S A LIE... HE MADE THAT UP...

HMMM.
SO WHAT DO YOU THINK?
CAN YOU GET ALONG?

NOT A CHANCE.
THIS GUY IS SCUM...

I'M GLAD YOU GUYS ARE HITTING IT OFF.

I'M PUTTING DENJI IN YOUR SQUAD, HAYAKAWA.

Squad?
THIS THUG?! REALLY?!

BUT WE ALREADY HAVE SO MANY TROUBLE-MAKERS AS IT IS!
IF WE ADD ANY MORE WEIRDOS...

I TOLD YOU WHEN WE CREATED YOUR SQUAD, DIDN'T I?
THAT I'D TRY OPERATING IT WITH A UNIQUE EXPERIMENTAL SETUP.

YAWN

JUST WHO IS THIS GUY?

DENJI HERE IS HUMAN, BUT HE CAN TURN INTO A DEVIL.

HOW DO YOU LIKE THAT?! BADASS, RIGHT?!

ARE YOU SERIOUS?
I'VE ONLY HEARD FLIMSY RUMORS ABOUT CASES LIKE THAT...

DENJI IS SPECIAL.
SO IT'S BEEN DECIDED THAT WE'LL TREAT HIM AS A SPECIAL CASE.

IF DENJI EVER QUITS OR DISOBEYS ORDERS...
...HE'LL BE PUT DOWN AS A DEVIL.

IT MEANS WE'LL BE WORKING TOGETHER UNTIL DEATH DO US PART.

WAIT... WHAT'S THAT MEAN?

本ビル
タツキバンク

TURNS OUT YOU'RE GONNA LIVE WITH ME SO WE CAN KEEP AN EYE ON YOU.
FYI, THEY TOLD ME I CAN KILL YOU IF YOU RUN AWAY.

HEY...
IS MAKIMA A BAD PERSON?

IF YOU THINK SO, THEN GIVE UP ON HER.

IF YOU'RE A DEVIL, JUST BE GRATEFUL WE'RE LETTING YOU LIVE.
WE'RE DEVIL HUNTERS, REMEMBER?

THEN IS SHE A GOOD PERSON?

OF COURSE SHE'S A GOOD PERSON...
I OWE HER MY LIFE...

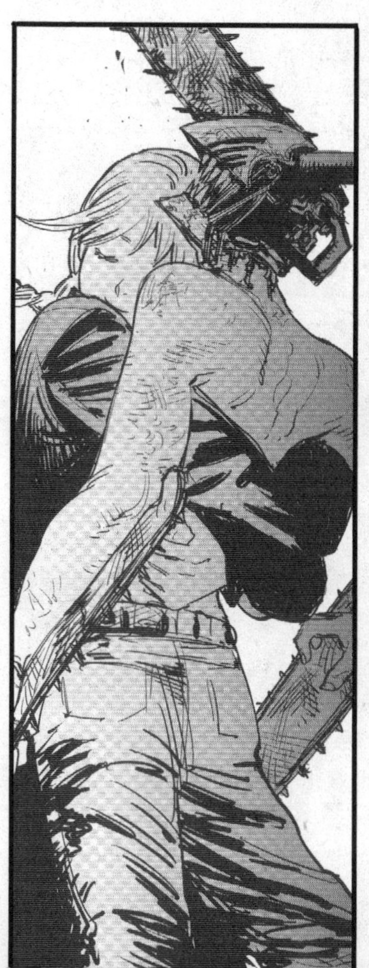

I WANNA HUG HER AGAIN.

Say what?!

Chain
saw
man

Chapter 4: Power

STRAWBERRY JAM, PLUM JAM, MARMALADE AAAND...
いちご
うめ

...BUTTER AND HONEYYY AND... SHAKE SOME CINNAMON ON THERE TOO.
ハチミツ大好
牛バター

TA-DAA
AND THE ULTIMATE BREAD IS READY!

Mm!

66

UNION JOB, HUMM HUH-HUMM HUH HUH HUH HUH-HUMMM!
PAID DAYS OFF, HUH-HUMM HUH-HUMM-HUM HUH-HUMM HUH-HUMMM HUM!
YOU'RE TAKING TOO LONG IN THE BATH!
bam
bam
bam

DON'T SLEEP ON THE TOILET!

WE'VE GOT A *FIEND* INSIDE AN EAST NERIMA RESIDENCE.
CIVILIAN EVACUATION AND LOCKDOWN OF THE SCENE IS COMPLETE AT THIS TIME.

THE FIEND TARGET IS HOLED UP IN A ROOM ON THE SECOND FLOOR.
WE'LL LET YOU DEVIL HUNTERS HANDLE THE REST.
MR. HAYAKAWA, IS THAT A NEWBIE WITH YOU?

HEY, WHAT'S A FIEND?

WHAT? DIDN'T YOU LEARN ANYTHING IN SCHOOL?
NOPE, DIDN'T GO TO SCHOOL.

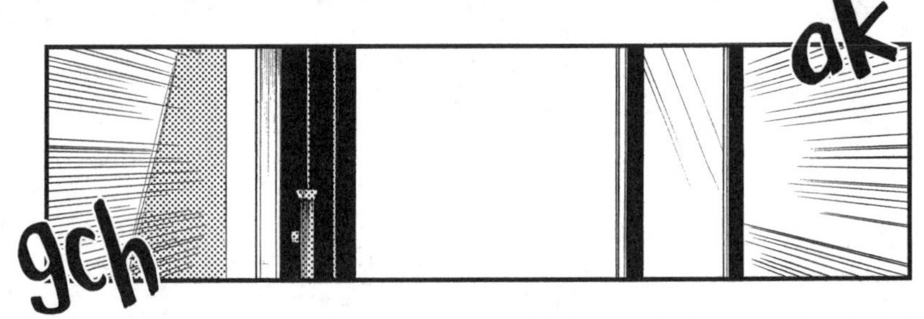
gch
ak

A DEVIL THAT'S TAKEN OVER A PERSON'S CORPSE...
THAT'S A FIEND.

OH REALLY? UH...
OHH.
THEN AREN'T I ONE?

NO.
THEIR HEADS HAVE DISTINCT SHAPES.

WELL, YOU'LL UNDERSTAND WHEN YOU SEE ONE.

WH
AM

FIENDS HAVE THE DEVIL'S PERSON-ALITY.
YOU KILL THIS ONE.

TURN INTO A DEVIL. SHOW ME YOUR POWER.
I'LL DECIDE WHETHER YOU'RE USE-FUL OR NOT.

DON'T LOOK! I'LL KILL YOU! I'LL KILL YOU! I'LL KILL YOU DEVIL HUNTERS!

HEY.
WHY DIDN'T YOU USE YOUR DEVIL POWER?

BANG

LISTEN UP. DON'T YOU FORGET THIS.

FIENDS ARE BONA FIDE DEVILS TOO.

A DEVIL HUNTER SHOULDN'T BE SYMPATHIZING WITH DEVILS.

EVERYONE IS SERIOUS ABOUT THIS BUT YOU.
I WANT TO KILL DEVILS IN WAYS THAT CAUSE THEM TO SUFFER AS MUCH AS POSSIBLE.
WHAT DO YOU WANT? TO BE FRIENDS WITH THEM?

IF THERE ARE DEVILS I COULD BE FRIENDS WITH, THEN YEAH, I DO.
CUZ I DON'T HAVE ANY FRIENDS...

I'LL REMEMBER THOSE WORDS...
Slam

BLAAAH... HE SURE HAS A SHORT TEMPER...

THE TRUTH IS, I JUST DIDN'T WANNA GET BLOOD ON THESE DIRTY MAGAZINES...

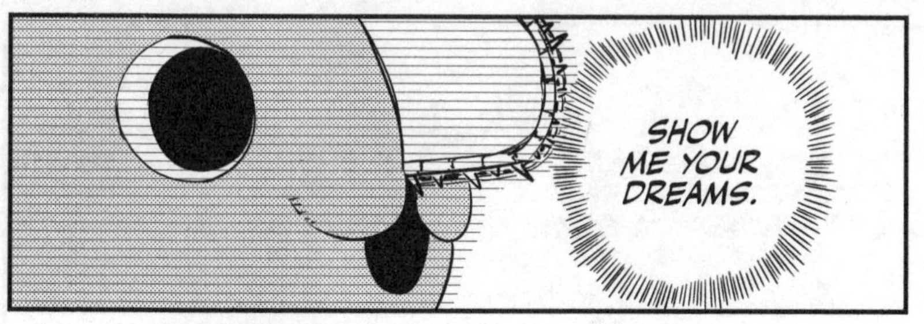
SHOW ME YOUR DREAMS.

I'M SERIOUS ABOUT THIS TOO, POCHITA.
I'M LIVING A DREAM LIFE, JUST LIKE IN OUR CONTRACT, AREN'T I?

IT'S JUST THAT I'VE ALREADY CROSSED THE FINISH LINE TO MY DREAM.
HE'S STILL CHASING HIS.

I GET
TO BATHE
EVERY
DAY.
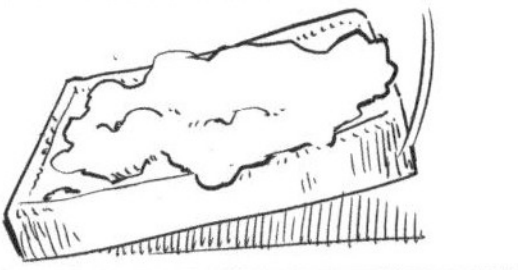
AND EAT
GOOD
FOOD.

WITH A
PRETTY
GIRL
CLOSE
BY...

I HAVE A FULL
LIFE NOW...
BUT IT DOES
KINDA FEEL LIKE
SOMETHING'S
MISSING.
WAS THERE
SOMETHING
ELSE?
MY REAL,
TRUE
GOAL...?

I BET HIS
ULTIMATE
GOAL IS A
REVENGE
THING.

FOR THE
GUYS BELOW,
IT'S PROTECTING
THEIR
FAMILIES.

DOES
MAKIMA
HAVE
ONE
TOO?

DOES
MAKIMA
ALSO...

I WANNA
TOUCH SOME
BOOBS...

I GAVE UP ON IT FOREVER AGO CUZ I THOUGHT IT WAS IMPOSSIBLE FOR ME...
BUT I HAVE A DECENT JOB NOW. COULDN'T I DO IT?

JUMPING STRAIGHT TO SLEEPING WITH A WOMAN WOULD BE TOUGH FOR ME...
BUT IF IT'S BOOBS...
IF IT'S BOOBS, IF I'VE GOT A STRONG WILL AND INITIATIVE, COULDN'T I TOUCH THEM...?

EVERYONE IS SERIOUS ABOUT THIS BUT YOU.

SO THAT'S WHAT HE MEANT! I'VE FOUND IT, DUDE...
WHAT I'M SERIOUS ABOUT!
MY GOAL!
IT'S...!

MELONS!!

FRUIT?

I'M PAIRING YOU UP WITH A BUDDY STARTING TODAY.

A BUDDY ...?

MAKIMA SAID SHE LIKED ME... BUT...
...IF I ASK TO TOUCH HER CHEST, THERE'S A CHANCE SHE'LL HATE ME...

IN PUBLIC SAFETY, FOR SMALL-SCALE MISSIONS, PATROLLING AND SO ON, WE ACT IN PAIRS FOR SAFETY'S SAKE.
PERFECT TIMING— LOOKS LIKE YOUR BUDDY'S HERE.

BE CARE- FUL...
SHE'S A FIEND.

HEY, HEY, HEY!
GROVEL, HUMAN!!
MY NAME IS POWER!
ARE YOU MY BUDDY OR WHATEVER?!

POWER?!
YOUR NAME IS POWER ?!
WAIT, YOU'RE A FIEND?!
FIENDS CAN BE DEVIL HUNTERS ?!
Well, what-ever!!
Lookin' forward to workin' with ya!

Chainsaw man

Chapter 5:
A Way to Touch Some Boobs

HUMAN! HURRY UP AND LET ME KILL SOME-THING!

I THIRST FOR BLOOD!

I CAN FORGIVE SOME CRAZINESS AS LONG AS SHE'S PRETTY...

THE ISSUE IS HOW I'M GONNA TOUCH THOSE BOOBS...

FIENDS ARE TARGETS FOR EXTERMINATION, SAME AS DEVILS.
BUT POWER HAS HIGH MENTAL FACULTIES, SO I PUT HER IN HAYAKAWA'S SQUAD.

HER HORNS WILL ATTRACT ATTENTION, SO ONLY PATROL PLACES WITH LITTLE TRAFFIC.

IF YOU RUN INTO ANY CIVILIAN DEVIL HUNTERS, OR GET QUESTIONED BY THE POLICE...

We're with Public Safety Devil Extermination Special Division 4, sirrrs.

IF YOU TELL THEM THAT AND SHOW THEM YOUR BADGE, THEY SHOULD SCOWL AND LEAVE YOU ALONE.
AS I'VE SAID BEFORE, PUBLIC SAFETY DEVIL EXTERMINATION SPECIAL DIVISION 4 IS AN EXPERIMENTAL SQUAD.
IF IT CAN'T DELIVER RESULTS, THE HIGHER-UPS MIGHT BREAK IT UP AT ANY TIME.
YOU TWO KNOW WHAT WILL HAPPEN TO YOU THEN, RIGHT?

There aren't any Devils at all!

LIKELY BECAUSE OF *ME!*

BEFORE I BECAME A FIEND, I WAS A GREATLY FEARED DEVIL!
THE NOBODY DEVILS ALL FLEE FROM MY SCENT, I'M SURE!

WAIT, WHAT?!
THEN HOW ARE WE GOING TO DELIVER RESULTS?!

IF YOU HAVE ANY QUESTIONS, ASK HAYAKAWA.
HE'S THE ONE WHO PAIRED YOU TWO UP.

THAT JERK... HE SET ME UP, DIDN'T HE?!

HE TEAMED ME UP WITH POWER TO KEEP ME FROM SHOWING WHAT I GOT.
HE'S TRYING TO FORCE ME OUT!

I SMELL BLOOD!!

HEY! WHOA, WHOA, WHOA! WHERE DO YOU THINK YOU'RE GOING?!

SHE'S FAST!

FIGHT TIME! FIGHT TIME! BATTLE TIME!

VPP
HAIR WE GO!!
WE G

Nerima Station
THE SCENE IS LOCKED DOWN AND CIVILIANS ARE EVACUATED.
REQUESTING BACKUP AT NERIMA STATION.
IT'S THE SEA CUCUM-BER DEVIL.
SEA CUCUM-BER DEVIL.
HUH? I SAID...

THE SEA—
タウンページ
Nerima

—CUMBER
...
I DID IT! THE GLORY IS MINE!!
GA HA HA HA HA HA!!

Suda Books
Fried Chicken
家庭情報
IT'S CONSIDERED OBSTRUCTION OF JUSTICE WHEN A PUBLIC SAFETY HUNTER KILLS A DEVIL A CIVILIAN HUNTER IS ALREADY ENGAGED WITH.
NORMALLY, YOU'D GET ARRESTED FOR IT.
POWER, YOU NEED TO THINK A LITTLE MORE BEFORE YOU ACT.
AND YOU, DENJI, YOU NEED TO KEEP HER UNDER CONTROL.
REALLY? YOU'RE BLAMING ME TOO?

THISH—

THIS GUY SAID TO KILL IT, HE DID!

HUH ?!

I NEVER SAID THAT! NOT EVEN CLOSE!
YOU'RE REALLY GONNA LIE AND THROW ME UNDER THE BUS LIKE THAT?!
I'M NOT LYING!! HE SAID IT!!
THIS HUMAN COMMANDED ME TO KILL THE DEVIL!! IT'S TRUE!!
What a creep!
Seriously?! Miss Makima, this Devil is a liar!!
You should be arrested!! You're gonna get arrested for the crime of lying and defamery or whatever!!
NO!
THIS DECEIVER TOLD ME TO DO IT! DEVILS CAN'T LIE!
ONLY HUMANS LIE!!
That's not a thing!!
You're the proof, stupidface!! You lying liar!!
HUMANS TELL NASTY LIES! I ONLY DID AS I WAS TOLD, 'TIS TRUTH!!
Quit talkin' all weird to sound cooler than you are!!
It's so creepy!!

CAN YOU BE QUIET?

I-I CAN!
HUH...?!

GOOD GIRL, POWER.
HONESTLY, I DON'T REALLY CARE WHICH OF YOU WAS AT FAULT.
I WANT TO SEE BIG THINGS FROM YOU TWO.

DO YOU THINK YOU CAN SHOW ME THAT?

I'LL SH—! SH-SHOW YOU!

MAYBE THIS ISN'T THE TIME TO BE THINKING ABOUT TOUCHING BOOBS.

Meooow!

GETTING TO HAVE SOFT DRINKS IS, LIKE, A DREAM COME TRUE TO ME.
BUT IF WE KEEP SCREWING UP, IT'LL BE WAY WORSE THAN NOT GETTING TO HAVE SOFT DRINKS ANYMORE!

STILL, I CAN'T WORK WITH SOME LIAR CHICK...

I HATE HUMANS!

NOT BECAUSE THEY DID ANYTHING TO ME.

IT'S LIKE A DEVIL INSTINCT. I JUST DO.

AND I HATE DEVILS TOO.

BECAUSE A DEVIL MADE OFF WITH MY PET, MEOWY!

I CAN ONLY GET ALONG WITH CATS.

MAKIMA CAUGHT ME BEFORE I COULD GET MEOWY BACK.

MEOWY MIGHT ALREADY BE DEAD, BUT I CAN'T GIVE UP.

IF I COULD JUST GET MEOWY BACK FROM THAT DEVIL, I'D DO ANYTHING— EVEN ALLY WITH A HUMAN!
I DOUBT YOU'D UNDERSTAND SUCH SENTIMENT FOR THE LIKES OF A CAT.

FOR A CAT? THAT'S STUPID!
I'D DO ANYTHING TO TOUCH SOME BOOBS THOUGH.

SURE ENOUGH, I CAN'T COMPREHEND HUMANS.

HMM ...
OH, BUT IF IT WAS A *DOG*, I MIGHT GET IT...

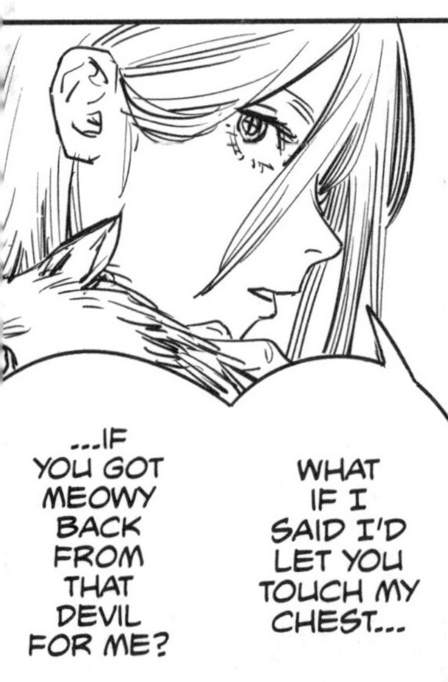
WHAT IF I SAID I'D LET YOU TOUCH MY CHEST...
...IF YOU GOT MEOWY BACK FROM THAT DEVIL FOR ME?

THAT DAMN DEVIL!

OHH?

HOW DARE...
...THEY KIDNAP A POOR CAT!!
OHH?!

THAT'S TOTALLY UNFOR-GIVABLE, RIGHT?!
YEAH!!
AS A DEVIL HUNTER, I CAN'T LET 'EM GET AWAY WITH IT!!
YEAH!!
I'LL MURDERIZE THAT DEVIL!!

Chain
saw
man

Chapter 6: Service

I KNOW WHERE TO FIND THE DEVIL WHO TOOK MEOWY!

THE PROBLEM IS THAT ONLY *YOU* CAN FIGHT IT.

IF IT SEES *ME*, IT'LL USE MEOWY AS A SHIELD.

THEN IT WOULD BE CHECK-MATE!

I CAN'T EVER PET HIM AGAIN, BUT IT'S OKAY.
CUZ HE'S ALIVE INSIDE ME, RIGHT IN HERE!
HUMANS ARE SO FOOLISH!

I HAD A PET TOO. THIS DEVIL NAMED POCHITA.

SAY WHAT?

THAT MEANS POCHITA DIED, DOES IT NOT?
THE DEAD HAVE NO LIFE!
"THEY'RE IN MY HEART" OR WHATEVER—THAT'S PATHETIC CONSOLATION!

Chapter 6: Service

THE SOVIET WAR HAWKS ARE GETTING LOUDER OVER THE AMERICAN MATTER.
WE'RE ALSO HEARING RUMORS THAT THEY'RE USING DEVILS FOR MILITARY PURPOSES.

WE CAN ONLY PRAY THAT THE DEVILS REMAIN JAPAN'S ONLY ENEMIES.
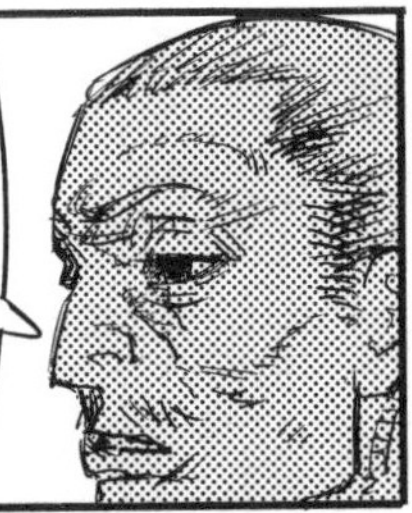
MAKIMA... ARE THE DOGS IN THE SQUAD WE GAVE YOU COMING ALONG...?

I HAVE ONE DOG THAT'S PROMIS-ING...
...AND ONE THAT'S INTER-ESTING.

INTER-ESTING ...?

A PUPPY I RECENTLY TOOK IN.

ta
p

YOUR JOB IS TO TRAIN DOGS AND USE THEM.
BE SURE NOT TO GET ATTACHED.

SL
AM

DENJI IS DISGUSTING. THERE'S NOTHING INTERESTING ABOUT HIM.
WHY DO YOU HAVE SUCH HIGH HOPES FOR HIM?

ALL DEVILS ARE BORN WITH A NAME.

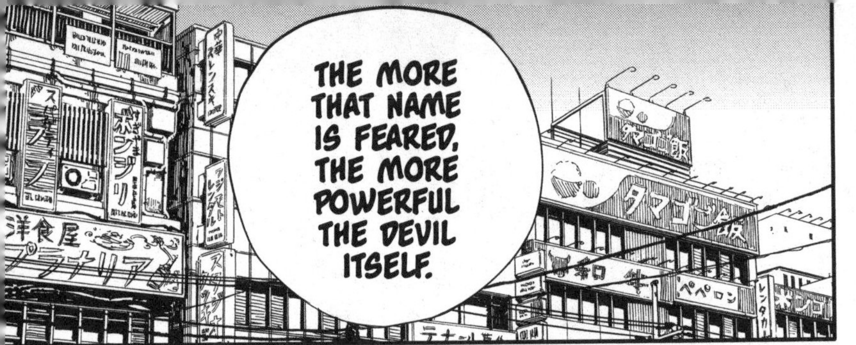
THE MORE THAT NAME IS FEARED, THE MORE POWERFUL THE DEVIL ITSELF.
洋食屋
ペペロン

COFFEE HAS NO SCARY MENTAL IMAGE WHATSOEVER. IF THERE WAS A *COFFEE DEVIL,* IT WOULD PROBABLY BE WEAK.

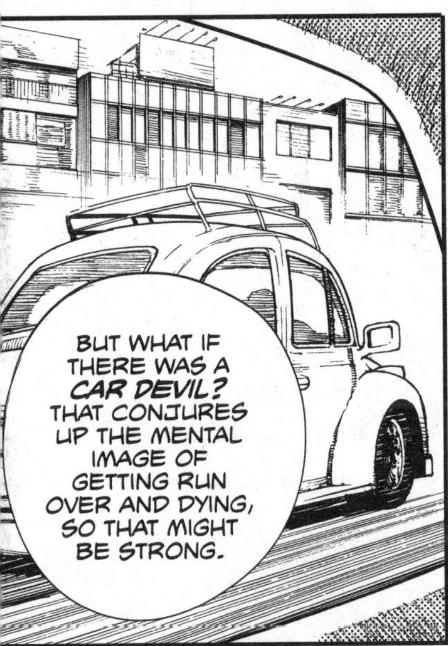
BUT WHAT IF THERE WAS A *CAR DEVIL?* THAT CONJURES UP THE MENTAL IMAGE OF GETTING RUN OVER AND DYING, SO THAT MIGHT BE STRONG.

DENJI CAN TURN INTO THE *CHAINSAW DEVIL.*

IT'S INTERESTING AND NOTHING MORE. HE'S USE-LESS.

'TIS THAT HOUSE!

MEOWY AND THE DEVIL ARE IN THERE!

HUUUH... THEN LET'S GET OUR BUTTS OVER THERE.

HUMAN JESTS ARE SO UNAMUS-ING!

HUH?

YEAH? WHAT IS IT?

A SLIP OF THE TONGUE...
...IT WAS.
FWSH
SHR

WHAM
AH!

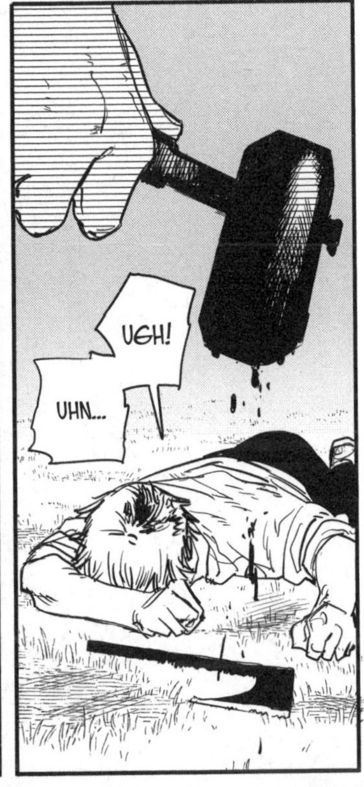

YOU MADE ME WAIT FOR QUITE SOME TIME, BLOOD DEVIL...

I THOUGHT YOU'D RUN AWAY...

SLAM

DON'T COM-PLAIN!

I HAD TO WAIT THAT LONG TILL I COULD FINALLY GET OUTSIDE TOO!

MY FIRST MEAL IN SO LONG!

A YOUNG MALE, EH...? LOOKS LIKE I'LL GET TO DRINK BLOOD BRIMMING WITH LIFE FORCE!

GAH!

LOOK AT MY ARM, HUMAN! YOU DAMN HUMANS DID THIS TO ME!
THIS INFERNAL WOUND FORCED ME TO HIDE MY GRAND SELF!

LIKE I CARE, IDIOT!

MY MEAL BARKS!

HUMANS CARVED THIS WOUND UPON ME...
...SO I'LL HEAL IT WITH HUMAN BLOOD!

GYAAAAAAAH!!
H
HRN?! YOU TASTE DISGUSTING!!
SP
LAT

NOW I'VE GONE AND REGEN-ERATED ...
...FROM DISGUSTING BLOOD BECAUSE OF YOUUU!!

WHAT A REVOLTING TASTE!!
I'LL HAVE TO EAT OTHER HUMANS TO GET RID OF THIS TASTE!
THUMP

WHAT DO YOU WANT? TO BE FRIENDS WITH DEVILS?
I CAN'T BELIEVE YOU TOOK MY STORY FOR TRUTH.
HUMANS REALLY ARE FOOLISH.

Chainsawman

Chapter 7: Meowy's Whereabouts

NOW THAT'S NOT A BAD SMELL.

I'VE SETTLED ON CHILDREN TO CLEANSE MY PALATE!

BAT DEVIL !!

I BROUGHT YOU A HUMAN AS PROMISED!
NOW GIVE MEOWY BACK!

HRRM ?
AH, YES... WAS THAT THE DEAL?

Mroow!
MEOWY!!
Myah! Myah!
BUT I STILL HAVEN'T PUNISHED YOU FOR BRINGING ME DISGUSTING BLOOD, HAVE I?

Mrow!
MEOWY...

MEOWY!
YOUR NAME SHALL BE MEOWY!
FOR A CAT, YOU SMELL TASTY!

lick

spssh

HURRY AND GROW BIG!
I'M EAGER TO KILL YOU!

Meoooow.

I'VE ALWAYS KILLED EVERYTHING THAT MET MY GAZE...
IT FEELS STRANGE TO HEAR A VOICE THAT ISN'T SCREAM-ING...
SO STRANGE ...
BLOOD DEVIL!

Meeew!

gulp

YOU SAID YOU CAN'T PET POCHITA ANYMORE...

I KNOW HOW YOU FEEL.
'TIS AN AWFUL FEELING, ISN'T IT?
GSH

GULP
DIS-
GUST-
ING!
NOTHING
BUT
DISGUSTING
BLOOD!
GRRNGH!

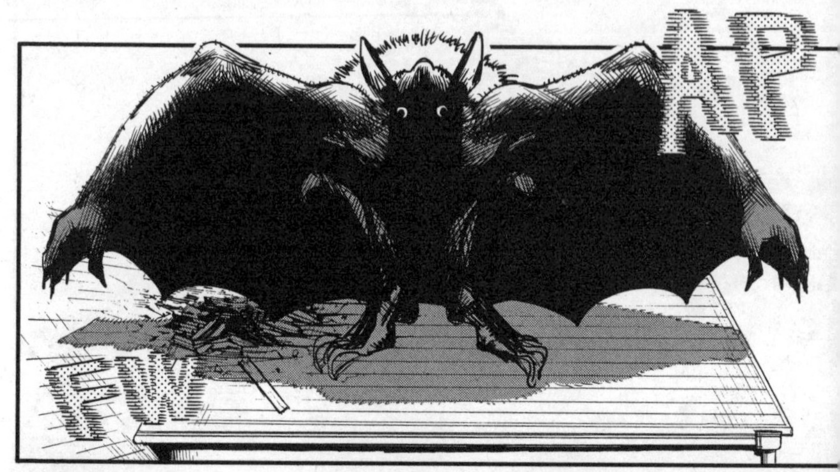

KRA
SH

GAAH! MY MOUTH TASTES REVOLTING!

I MUST RINSE IT OUT WITH THE BLOOD OF CHILDREN!

AFTER I'VE GARGLED, I'LL HAVE A VIRGIN AS AN APPETIZER.
FOR THE SOUP, A HEALTHY WOMAN OF RIPE AGE.
THE MAIN COURSE WILL BE A GOOD, PLUMP MAN.
AND FOR DESSERT, I DESIRE A PREGNANT WOMAN!
HRRN?

GIMME BACK MY BOOBS!
YOU'RE DRINKING MY BLOOD...?! HOW VILE!
I DO NOT HAVE ANY DESIRE TO DRINK *YOUR* BLOOD!

SNAP
KRAK
KRAK
SNAP

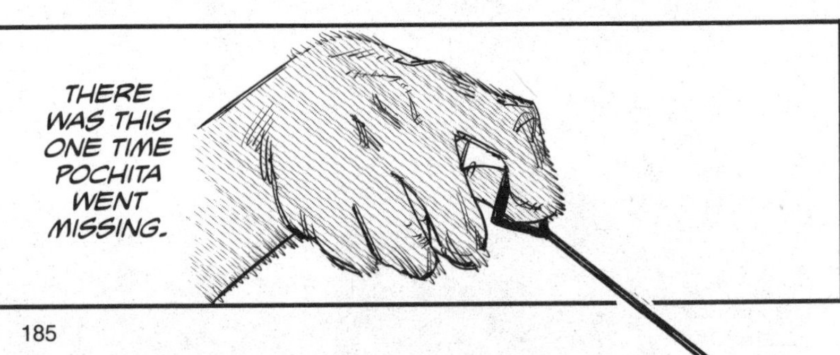
THERE WAS THIS ONE TIME POCHITA WENT MISSING.

AFTER MEOWY GOT TAKEN BY A DEVIL...

...HOW DID SHE FEEL WHEN SHE WENT TO SLEEP AT NIGHT?

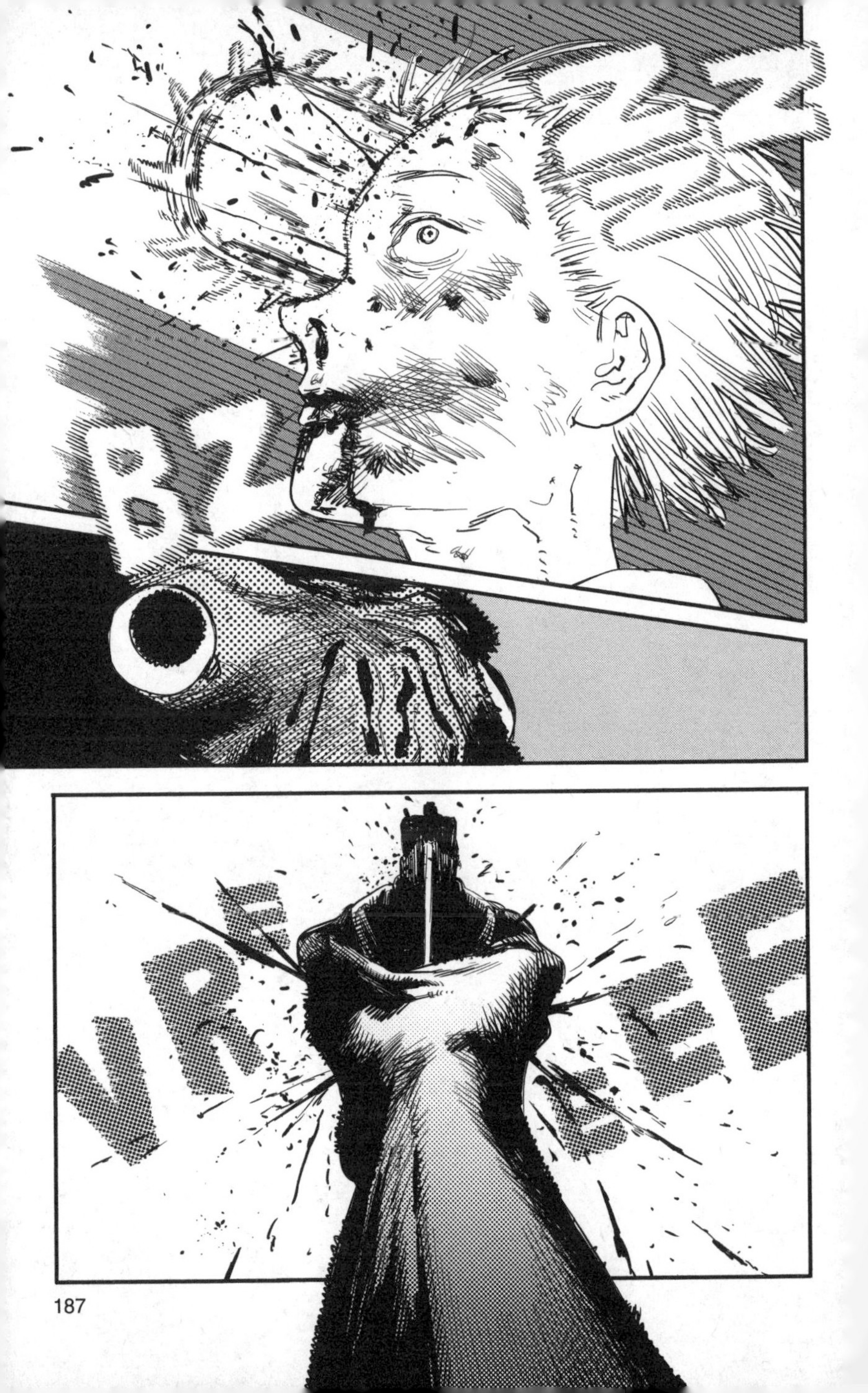

BZ
ZZZ
VR
EEE

TO BE CONTINUED...

Chain
saw
man

HEY, DON'T THROW AWAY YOUR APPLE PEELS.
THESE ARE EDIBLE!
IF YOU DON'T WANT THE SKIN, GIVE IT TO ME.
I'LL EAT IT.
GIMME YOUR SCABS.
I CAN EAT THOSE.
NO WAY.
WHY NOT?! THEY'RE NUTRI-TIOUS!
WHAT KIND OF LIFE HAVE YOU LIVED?

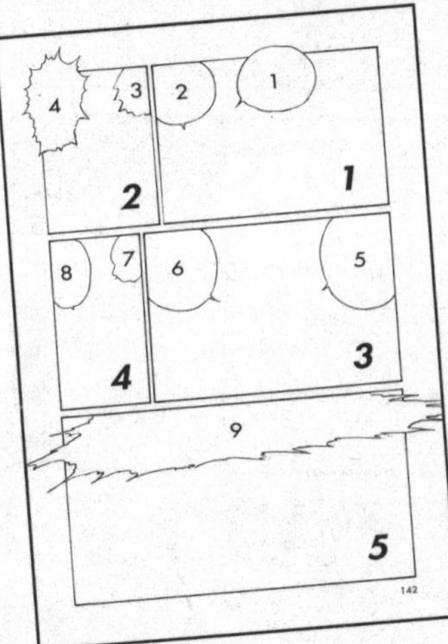

Chainsaw Man reads from right to left, starting in the upper-right corner. Japanese is read from right to left, meaning that action, sound effects and word-balloon order are completely reversed from English order.